GHOUL:

WAGHZEN

Kathleen Woolrich

with a contribution of Sophia Laila Agag

Kathleen Woolrich Books
2019

First Printing: 2019

ISBN: 978-0-578-22764-1

Kathleen Woolrich Books
2125 Shaffer Pl,
Orlando, FL 32806, USA

Dedication

Kathleen Voss Woolrich is the mother of 4, one deceased and has travelled to Algeria 10 times and lived there in the winter of 2015 2016. She has written several books including MARTYR, ALGERIAN SUNS and SLAVES of ALGIERS. She has devoted her life to helping North African immigrants with support, housing care and their emergency needs. GHOUL is a poetry book that focuses on several friendships and love stories she has had with Algerians. This book was written in the summer of 2019 in New York City and across Algeria. You can reach her at kwoolr@aol.com or via facebook at Kathleen Voss Woolrich

Sophia Laila Agag is the daughter of a an Italian American beauty and her father is from Tizi Rached Algeria. She works tirelessly to help the Algerian American community and is a graduate student at Baruch College

Contents

The end of the story and no longer my ghoul

As I close my eyes I think of you
I said goodbye a thousand times
You refused to let me love you
You refused to tell me your truth
So I will get in my car and drive away from you
Into the wind I'll leave you because I can't reach you anymore
Before I go, I'll say everything I need to tell you
I'll tell you how much I loved you
I'll brush my hair and let it down
I'll kiss your nose and your face and your forehead
I'll tell you I am sorry for being angry or hurt
I'll let you know that you were everything
And I'll end the story and the book with love
This is the last poem of ghoul
This is the end of me and you and our story
Now baby... I have nothing left to say
I have exorcised my demons and I am letting you go
You don't have to be kind to me or hold on to me
I am a memory in your mind and I wish you only we
You'll find me in the ocean and in the stars and every where
And you will know I loved you so
This is the end of our story beloved
This is the end of the summer of 2019
There is nothing left to say.
Except baby I love you
Nothing left to tell you
I am driving away into the sunlight and I will dance in the water
and remember you
I will remember you
The way the light hit your eyes
The way your skin felt under my hands
And I will close my eyes and dream of you
I remember you with love and kindness
I wish you sunlight and wind behind you
I wish you happiness at every turn
You are no longer my ghoul

You are my memory

Summer never lasts.

by Sophia Laila Agag

Just like the time we shared. The hot African sun shining in your gorgeous green eyes, like emerald gems. Your precious smile that hypnotizes me. I felt safe as you guarded me on every step I took next to you. You replaced back emotions that were missing for years, feelings that I believed were gone. It's hard to let you go and move on with my days without you. The distance is so painful and unbearable. I am not sure what i am feeling but it's taken over my entire my mind and heart. But, did I only dream for it being true? Only time can tell... I hope I can see your smile again one day.

Ghoul (ROULA)

The one I love is cruel
The one I love is a ghoul
The winds have taken him
And left behind a monster who walks the streets
Looking for the next victim
To bite her neck and leave his venom
The one I love is cruel
The one I love is a predator
He looks for white hearts and stabs them and torments them
The one I love is heartless
he's a ghoul with the softest skin and eyes like the moon
He walks the streets at night like a ghoul
And breaks the hearts of the sweetest and kind
He died yesterday
The ghoul took his last breath yesterday
Now all he is a memory
we took his body to the cemetery
I threw stones upon his coffin
And turned to walk away
and I saw mist in the streets and the skies went black
The one I love is cruel
The one I love is unkind
But now he lays in a cemetery far away
His eyes no longer shine
He's just a battered book in a room I no longer enter.
On a shelf protected from destruction
But I'll never read from his book of shadows
I'll never ask for him or pray a prayer
For now he's dead to me
The one I love is cruel

The Maghreb

Are you waiting for me?
Ill lay everything on the ground
And break every wall to return to you
They might wait for me
And love me like I need to be loved
So wrap your arms around me
And let me come back to you
From the shores of Rabat to the waters of Azzefoun
I know you are waiting for me
I no longer care if it's logical or sensible
I will search for you in their eyes
I will look for you in every corner
The Maghreb haunts me
And I wake from sleep with no rest
My body aches and my limbs are broken
Until I return to you
The Maghreb

Did you feel it?

I let you go.
I am not holding your hand any more
I gave up on you
I am floating out to sea... I don't love you anymore
I let you go
I saw your ugly and I covered my eyes
And now I don't want to look at you anymore
I am not sure I even like you
Did you feel it? The moment I fell out of love with you

There was nothing else to love or look at
All I see is the blackness of your face and heart
My sunlight has left your street
Your selfishness covers up the green grass that grows in your
soul
So I had to leave

Baby did you feel it? Can you feel I fell of love with you?
My heart does not dance when I look in your eyes
I don t love you anymore and it can never come back
You have everything you dream of but not in my sunlight
I don t respect you any more
Baby do you feel it? Baby did you feel me leave
I let go of your hands
Baby do you feel it?

Underwater

by Sophia Laila Agag

Holding the world on my shoulders
Reaching out but rejected
Muffled voices
My heart collapses

Drowning underwater

Paralyzed while sinking
Cloudy sight turns dark
Torn between reality and fantasy
But my soul remains in my lifeless body.

Drowning underwater

washed up ashore
I regain consciousness
I forgive and accept what I have.
I feel strong and ready to fight again

Rising from underwater.

I lost it all

I lost my taste for food
I lost the blood in my arms and legs
I fell so hard for you
And now it's just nothing at all
It's less than a sentence
Just space on paper and my heart is so broken
Take everything you took from me and burn it or throw it
You broke everything inside of me
I just want to return to life before you
I take pills to sleep and wake in pain
Because there's nothing for me left in any of this
Nothing left for me in the words that I speak or the words that I
write about you
Because it's pointless to love a mirage
Spirit yourself away to anywhere you want
Kiss any face and love anyone
I just want to banish you from my heart and my mind
Because it's absolutely pointless to love you
I lost it all before you arrived and you left me in the negative
I lost it all beloved. I lost it all

Without you

It doesn't make it fair
Doesn't make it right
I love him and he doesn't see me
I did not decide to love him because I had answers
I loved him because he answered something inside me
From the first time his eyes met mine
And I knew
it doesn't make it fair or right
I'll never be with him
I am hopelessly devoted
Lost forever in the knowledge he exists
He doesn't love me back
but I love him enough for both or us
I had to let him go
And let my love just flow and pour upon the ground
He will never love me like I need
I'll probably cry a thousand tears for him
and maybe one day he will look
at something and remember me
without you beloved... beloved without you

For the mountain

I turned into a ghost
I spoke his name to the wind a couple of times
Then it was time to leave
I was like a star who spoke to him several times
But he could not see me
So I burned as hot as I could burn
Then I left the sky
I never burned again
I held a little love left inside my hands
I rubbed my hands together and knew I had to leave
There would be no more talks of books
I was not beautiful enough for him to read me
I took my broken parts and showed him everything
But I was not the ether or the salve that could save him
So just like that I let go of the rope
I let go of him and I won't come back
But some night when it's late at night
And nothing makes sense he might ask for me
And I won't be in the sky anymore or a shadow he is expecting.
Beauty is not what I was
A beautiful broken picture of who I used to be
I loved who he wasn't
He didn't know that I understood his loss
No one can fill a broken heart
Not time nor drink not time the loss revives itself
Loves martyr lies alone
Swimming in sheets that are cool
I disappeared and became a ghost
Like broken hearted lovers do

Broken hearted woman

I am a broken hearted woman
I pray for peace inside my eyes
But I buried my future...
And I rose like a phoenix
An angry queen
Do not come too close. I cannot contain
My tears of loss and terror
I need to be held till I cry it all out
I need to be cared for
And there's not enough love in this world to fix me
There's not enough time for me to cry
Not enough time to ease my pain
I am just a broken hearted woman
I am trapped in a garden of thorny roses
I can see beauty but I cannot have it for myself
And I buried my dreams like most lovers do
I am just a broken hearted woman

The end of the story and no longer my ghoul

As I close my eyes I think of you
I said goodbye a thousand times
You refused to let me love you
You refused to tell me your truth
So I will get in my car and drive away from you
Into the wind I'll leave you because I can't reach you anymore
Before I go, I'll say everything I need to tell you
I'll tell you how much I loved you
Ill brush my hair and let it down
Ill kiss your nose and your face and your forehead
I'll tell you I am sorry for being angry or hurt
I'll let you know that you were everything
And I'll end the story and the book with love
This is the last poem of ghoul
This is the end of me and you and our story
Now baby... I have nothing left to say
I have exorcised my demons and I am letting you go
You don't have to be kind to me or hold on to me
I am a memory in your mind and I wish you only happiness
You will find me in the ocean and in the stars and every where
And you will know I loved you so
This is the end of our story beloved
This is the end of the summer of 2019
There is nothing left to say.
Except baby I love you
Nothing left to tell you
I am driving away into the sunlight and I will dance in the water
and remember you
I will remember you
The way the light hit your eyes
The way your skin felt under my hands
And I will close my eyes and dream of you
I remember you with love and kindness
I wish you sunlight and wind behind you
I wish you happiness at every turn

You are no longer my ghoul
You are my memory

Ḥemlaɣ-k war aḥezzeb

translated by Sonia Ait Ahmed

Ḥemlaɣ-k am akken jellbeɣ ɣer ugaraw seddaw ugʷmam

Ḥemlaɣ-k almi tezziɣ Ur zmireɣ ak sɛuɣ Ur zriɣ ara anwa

ḥemleɣ Wissen ma d l'ADN ik hemleɣ?

Tura ugadaɣ-k Ḥemlaɣ-k war aḥezzeb Ḥemlaɣ-k war azekka
Ḥemlaɣ-k akken ttafɣeɣ

Amzun hesleɣ deg ugwens Ḥemlaɣ-k akken iy iqerreḥ w aḍu di
tbuciḍant

Ldiɣ tiwwura u ɣetseɣ ak hemleɣ

Ḥemlaɣ-k akken ur zmireɣ ara ad ḥulfuɣ idamen deg iɣallen iw

Ahat ma rriɣ-d nnefs si cwiṭ n tayri iy id iqqimen ad izmireɣ ak
ɛiwneɣ ad iliḍ tumred daɣen

Ahat ma fkiɣ ak ul iw fkiɣ ak cwiṭ seg wayen id iqqimen ad
izmireɣ ak selkeɣ seg unezgum Ad jemɛeɣ iceqfan yerzen w ak
id selkeɣ daɣen

Ḥemlaɣ-k war aḥezzeb Ḥemlaɣ-k akken ttezzin iẓuyaḍ

Nek mačči d win tebɣid neɣ tehwaǧeḍ Nek d win ig ṭfen di
leḥyuḍ n wexxam a Tɛeddin iẓuyaḍ zdat neɣ U nek ssawaleɣ s
ismi-k Izemrasen

Ḥemlaɣ-k war aḥezzeb

I love you so recklessly

I love you so recklessly
I love you like I jumped in the ocean and there is an undertow
I love you so much that I am spinning
And you aren't attainable
I am not even sure what I am in love with
Am I in love with your DNA?
I am now terrified of you
I love you so recklessly
I love you with no tomorrow. I love you like I am flying. Like I
sank into the floor boards
I love you like the wind hurts my face during a hurricane
I threw open the doors and decided just to love you
I love you like I cannot feel the blood go to my arms
Maybe if I breathe ever bit of love I have left in me. I can help
you be happy again
Maybe if I gave my heart to you... gave you what little I had left,
Id save you from sadness
I'd pick up the broken pieces.. Id save you and me at the same
time
I love you so recklessly
I love you like the storms are circling overhead
And I am not the one you want or need
But If I hold on to the walls of this house
And the storms swarm up ahead
And I call your name Izemrasen

Izemrasen
Beloved.
I love you so recklessly

The walls

Knock down the walls to get to me
I am sending out distress signals
Call my name and say you're coming for me and that I belong to
you
Say my name proudly and claim me. Say this is mine and I love
her
If you cannot do that, then I don't want you
I will love you but I will leave you
Leave the mountain and come for me, love and protect me
If you cannot leave your mountain, stay on it and I'll find my
way alone
If you cannot love me publicly and hold me, care for me and
honor me
Then keep your love. I do not want it
Keep your heart and keep your eyes
Keep your soul and keep our memories
If you cannot love me in front of the world, then keep your love.
Keep each kiss and keep each look
Be happy with everything you have
I love you but I am leaving. If you want me you know where to
find me
You either break these walls and carry me out of this burning
house
Or leave me to die in it
I am no one's secret
the walls
write my name on your skin and breathe my love into you
I am no one's secret
the walls darling the walls. I am holding onto the walls of the
house as the roof blows by
Because I know you won't come. I know you cannot
But you will know that I love you and you denied me

these walls

Iyad ɣer illel ay aserdas iw ḥemlaɣ-k

Iyad ɣer illel ay aserdas iw ḥemlaɣ-k
cḥal d abrid inniɣ iy iman iw
tayri agi isefk at nger
maca tafat n wallen ik ḍwant ul iw
iyad ɣer illel ay aserdas iw
Xas ur zmireɣ ak sɛuɣ zemreɣ ak waliɣ
ad nnaleɣ iḍuḍan ik an wali igenni d iselman ɣef yiri
nezmer anemmeslay zdat ugaraw w ad ḥṣuɣ tqerbeḍ ɣuri
ay aserdas iw
Ḥercawit iḍuḍan ik deg usemmiḍ
Isefk at iliḍ deg uẓwu yeḥman
tiẓeẓewt n tisent ɣef udem ik
Iyad ɣer illel ay aserdas iw innuɣnan
Deg uqrab iw llant tiɣawsiwin ak id selken
Taqerɛet n zzit iṭriḥin am lyasmin
adlis n isefra ay mmeslayen iw ul ik
zemreɣ ak id cnuɣ tizlit ar umeẓẓuɣ ik
iyad ɣer illel ay aserdas iw
anda anebdu ur itfaka
tzemreḍ d kečč ay
tzemreḍ d kečč ay iselken seg uqraḥ iw
selken seg uqraḥ iw
iyad ɣer illel a tayri w
iyad ɣer illel ay aserdas iw
Iyad ɣer illel Yugurten... iyad ɣer illel

Beautiful Soul

Beautiful soul
I lost the ability to talk to you.
I don't know how to tell you anything any more
It's nothing you did
But I can't find the words to tell you anything any more
I am filled with terror to speak to you
Beautiful soul
I see you
I know the nights you open your eyes and play back memories of her
I wish I could give you back the time that you need to live again
I am just so broken

O I have to run away from you beautiful soul

I have to pretend to myself I never knew you

I have to pretend to myself that I did not see deep inside

Everything you did not do... you did. You did everything good

You were perfect.

I saw you in my dreams beautiful soul

Beautiful soul I see you

Beautiful soul take good care of yourself

Beautiful soul... tell me one day you understand what I am saying to you

Beautiful soul

Love is a wine I cannot drink right now

Love is a wine I cannot drink right now
Massinissa my brother
I am unable to bring a glass to my lips
I cannot see eyes and shake from adoration
I cannot hold hands right now
Love is a wine I cannot drink right now
I cannot lift its boldness to my lips

I cannot lay under sheets and feel cool air brush my skin
Or be adored with my face held by strong hands. I might just
break in two

Love is a bitter wine for me... I tasted from the cup of love and
was thrown into a closet
And hurt and I swore I would emerge and dance in a fountain and
drink again
But love is a wine I cannot taste right now
The ground below me is not safe
The words spoken to me untrue
Desire is a lie and my heart is broken
Love is a wine I cannot drink right now

What made you change?

by Sophia Laila Agag

When I look through the dusty subway window passing through the decades-old tunnels, I think of your precious smile. I miss you every minute of my days. I dedicate my achievements for you, do you ever notice them? I am crazy for you, but I remain silent. Since you changed, it felt like a million thorns stuck in my heart. I should not let my heart speak over my mind. But why did you held me and let me go so quickly? I did not catch my balance. What made you change? I look back to my summer moments with you when I was blinded with non-existing love, I yelled in anger during the day and cried at night. What made you change? You are still attached to me, but we communicate like strangers with worthless words. I am tired of hiding my feelings, and you are taking over my mind. Letting go is painful, forgetting you is impossible.

Crucify

bend my body back
you held a knife to my throat
you bit me till I bled
I know you want to crucify me
I know you want to possess my soul
The first minute i met you i needed to run from you
your black eyes told me that you would be my psycho path
here I am to crucify
I took two pills and you killed me
You laid me down with my arms spread across the bed
All you did was crucify me
All you did was take my life

Now I am a ghost who follows you

You are the one who took my soul

The man who was so quiet the one who I loved

but he held secrets

Baby come take my everything

crucify

crucify

tie me to the stake and burn me

Burn down my house and burn down my life

I know you came to me to crucify

me

Only he could save me

Only he could save me
But I was too broken
Too shattered
I needed love he did not feel for me
Only he could save me
Only he could save me but there was too little time
I opened up the doors that had been slammed shut for 10 years
I reached a place I could breathe again
Only he could save me, but it was way too late
I had coded on the bed. My blood ran cold and I turned blue

I died that day in walk up apartment
the bottle of Irish whisky in the kitchen
whisky in my head and on my lips

He looked at me and said, you are a liar
when I said I just couldn't feel anything any more
You are a liar. You are a liar
I lied when I said I was strong
 I lied when I said I could do this alone
I needed each touch. I needed the rejection afterwards
And now I'm stripped to the bone... naked and exposed
With tears never stopping
I clung to the sheets and wrapped everything around me
I drown in the darkness
I loved him a messy kind of tragic love
A skinned knees kind of love where it hurts so bad but you
needed to ride your bike so fast that you crashed
The heady pulse of Irish whiskey on my lips
with tears in my eyes that won't stop escaping
Only he could save me

Netlethiyi guer iguelidhen ts guellidhine

Bury me with the kings and the queens
translation by Lil lakhel

Netlethiyi guer iguelidhen ts guellidhine Bury me with the kings and the queens
T hulfugh swoliw youdhene .Vghigh ayindhene dhekchallik achevhane ayawine ar w akal , nelzayer
Ayijen arthama nlavhar marayghalli yitij sthawrikine netejra ayighoumene

Ourelligh segsen , nouthni iguelane sgui lahvaviw izayriyene
Th merreth lhalaw ala amenni iyidyougrane
Th merrath l halaw ala assirem iyidyougrane

You drifted away

I said good bye to you

I let go of your memory

Your eyes no longer penetrate mine

You are a picture in a book I cannot bear to read

I still remember you and love you

But I learned to live without you

You are no longer a living being

You are just foam on the ocean

You are a page in a book I put under my bed beloved

I placed you on a little boat

And you drifted away. , way out to sea

You are gone from my life beloved

You are just a memory

You drifted

away

Hurricane Heart

Winds come and blow the trees
Tear up the streets and hit the sides of my house
I have a hurricane heart
He broke everything inside of me when he said goodbye
Now if the winds come and tear everything shred to shred
Now the outside will look how my insides feel
Wind and water and my life turned upside down
I have a hurricane heart
I cannot be with him but I'm struggling to want to be with any-
one else
So I'll find my peace inside the hurricane
Ill face the wind and let the waters drown me

As high winds approach I won't be afraid

Because He tore what was left of me out of my chest

Baby's got a hurricane heart... My love was bigger than any fear

But I was only a side attraction, a joke and a distraction

He came ashore into my life and blew the doors open only to
leave me confused and lost

I have a hurricane heart... torn from one end to the other... its
holding on by tatters

I know I have to survive him. I just don't know how

How Do I put my heart back in my chest when he did not deserve
it to begin with?

He's evil and cold and never cared about me... I just want the
spell to be broken

I want the winds to scare the living pain out of me

I want the pills to sooth my tears and give me back my stability

I want him to disappear into the winds and for any trace of him to die inside of me

My poor battered... deceived and betrayed hurricane heart

All he did was lie and lie and stole what was left of me

I have a hurricane heart

Ala neṯṯa ig zemren ay isellek

translated by Sonia Ait Ahmed

ala neṯṯa ig zemren ay isellek
maca lliɣ ṛẓeɣ ffudiɣ
ḥwaĝeɣ tayri tin ur s iḥulfa
ala neṯṯa ig zemren ay isellek
ala neṯṯa ig zemren ay isellek maca ulac aṯṯas n wakud
ldiɣ d tiwwura ig medlen igɣelqen 10 iseggwasen
Wwḍeɣ s amkan anda zemreɣ ad rreɣ nnefs i tikelt nniḍen
ala neṯṯa ig zemren ay id isellek maca ifat lḥal ẓẓleɣ deg usu
idamen
ẓẓleɣ deg usu idamen iw ṣemḍit uɣaleɣ d tazegzawt
mmuteɣ assen deg uxxam
taqerɛeṯ n crab di tnawalt
crab deg uqerruy iw akw d icenfiren iw
immuql iy id yennad kem d takeddabt kem d takeddabt
imi id nniɣ ulac dacu iṯḥulfuɣ dayen
kem d takeddabt kem d takeddabt
skadbeɣ imi id nniɣ ĝehdeɣ
skadbeɣ imi zemreɣ ad xedmeɣ kullec waḥdi
ctaqeɣ yal annal ctaqeɣ yal tugin ik deffir waya
tura kkaweɣ almi d adif ɛeryan
skanayeɣ d imeṯṯawen iw yugin ad kfun
jgugleɣ deg ibellaṣen sburreɣ iman iw s yal taɣawsa
zedreɣ di tebrek ḥemleɣ t am tayri nni yumsen takesnant
tayri n tgucrar tunḥifin yeknan
tayri qerriḥen am ticki tebɣiḍ ad sedduḍ asinzi s tɣawalt syin at
sehwuḍ
d iḥulfuten iqwan n le whyskey ɣef icenfiren iw d imeṯṯawen ur
nḥebbes deg iẓr iw ala neṯṯa ig zemren ay isellek

Oh to love me like I love you

I'd cook every meal for you
I'd shop for the things you like
I'd wash your clothes and fold them and put them away
I'd make everything you needed close to you
If I could pull the moon down from the sky and hand it to you
beloved
You are lost in a world of people who don't understand you
I wish could give you everything you needed
Help you fill your dreams and be as big as you wanted
I wonder how long I have to wait to be with you
I wonder if it will ever be possible
To hold your face and make things right
You need every meal made for you with love and care
And your lunch packed and someone looking out for you
When you are sick and suffering
I love you so beloved
I lay alone so far from you and you can't see me
But in my dreams you hold me
In my dreams you see me and you touch my lips
And talk to me and understand me
My moon when can I be yours
My moon when can you see how much I love you
Maybe some days for you it is a joke
But the day your lips met mine I knew
I knew the sun rose and set in your eyes
I cannot replace you, I have tried every day
I have tried to hate you
But in the end.., even in my darkest hour
I reach for you. I reach for you
I long for you with all my heart
There is no other... my ghost

Chaba9tni ma9rout

I am full
I heard it all
My eyes cannot hold the tears
My head is spinning
I am trying to catch my balance
Chaba9tni ma9rout oumri
Chaba9tni ma9rout oumri

At the bottom of his glass

I know he saw me
He was drinking for about an hour
And I appeared in the ice beside the whiskey
Baby it's me, I am at the bottom of your glass
I am the one who was going to love you
I am the one who would give you peace
that the whiskey just can't bring
I am at the bottom of your glass baby
I am at the end of every drunken night
When you just want to talk and not be alone
I'd rather have a part of you than none of you
Please love me again
At the bottom of your glass, that's where my face lies
at the bottom of your glass, you can feel my hips under you
and you can kiss my face again
at the bottom of your glass, there I am again and I love you still
And no one can hurt you anymore
and the whiskey cannot cure what ails you
at the bottom of your glass , among the melted ice
It's a heady combination me and you and whiskey too
You can drink me like a tonic... and see my face when you set the
glass down
You can see me in the glass and feel me all around you
love is the strongest spirit and it will not disappear
at the bottom of the glass, I lay amongst the pieces
of the drink that you were drinking
and the smell of cigars creates my shape and you can see me in
the smoke that rises up from the ashtray
at the bottom of your glass baby, as you drink away your pain I
am next to you always
at the bottom of your glass

I hope every hand that touches you

I hope every kiss that lands upon your face is tender
I hope every hand that touches you has the softness of mine
I hope she's gentle with you and makes you everything you love
to eat
I'll never be that queen for you
Because you can't see me
All you see is broken and All I am is a queen
If you look at the outside
But if you saw my love inside
You'd see the sky in my eyes
You'd know I have all the answers for you and me
But I all I can do is wish wherever you land
That you land in tenderness
That every broken place is healed and that you feel real love
Real love doesn't own and still gives and cares
I locked my heart inside a cage
I saw your mistakes and I decided that I loved you enough for
both of us
You will never be there, never love me, never lie in my arms
But I want this for you
I want every woman who kisses you to put her hands in your hair
I want every pain you have inside to heal like a solid shield
You will always be the king of my heart
An Altar of love I will build at your feet
Step swiftly beloved
Here's a sword and shield to keep you safe
And one day, when you decide you have seen enough
I'll light my candle in my window to lead you back to me
I built your altar near my door step
With a candle in the window to bring you home
With a candle in a window to bring you home

Izem

His Eyes

His eyes have seen too much
His heart broke too completely
I love him but all I can do is stand outside
He will not allow me in
I gave up on his mountains
I gave up on his kiss
I closed my eyes and cannot look at him anymore
I died in his arms and I became lost in his eyes
His eyes

Bury me with the kings and queens

I suffer so from my sick heart
But in my heart
I want them to wrap me up in white cloth and carry me
and put me in the ground in Algeria
put me by the sea
leave me with the sunsets of the coast
and let the leaves of the trees cover me
I am not theirs but they are mine my beloved Algerians
So as things get harder for me I can only dream
When I leave this earth I return to Algerie
In a simple cloth wrapped so tight
with my body calm and free of pain
Leave me with my nieces and nephew
My beloved Algerians leave me at their side
So sometimes they can come and visit me
And say we loved her so

Leave my body in Algerie
Free of heart break and free of pain
Deliver me to the place that I feel peace
My people beloved Algerie
In Algerie I walk again I breathe ok I feel complete
My mind spins and all I want is to be reunited with her

So carry me to Algerie the bled my mother
the beloved white queen
And leave me forever with my people
Leave me with the kings and queens of Algeria and the warmest
sun
If I close my eyes come for me
Never leave me my babies my friends
My love goes on forever
Bury me with the kings and queens
bury me in Algeria

Thimouchouha

I want to tell a story
of when I loved you and you loved me
and all we had was the air in the room
and the days that left us... they have all grown cold

I want to tell a story
Of Jugurtha
And Massinissa and Kahina
and a million days gone by
and I could walk down from the mountain and burn all the trees
And imagine I am a queen and the hills were on fire

thimouchouha

and a million words between us
I could love you but I will not
I could remember but I cannot
I will just burn all the hills and cast myself off a cliff

And tell myself thimouchouha
Till I sleep
and grieve and tumble down the hills

thimouchouha

Themushuha

Avghigh akhdinigh thamacahout.
Ghaf Assan asmi nemyahmal
Ghafasmi ournass3i ala thakhamth ifarghan ,
Ouk thoussan ighyajane rouhan.
Yeqimd oukham dhassamadh,
Avghigh akhdahkough
Thamachahout anjugurtha
Thamachahout an massinissa
Thamachahout an kahina.
Thamachahout na boussane ighyajane rouhen,
......
Avghir awandahkugh themushuha

I cried for you

I would have packed my bags and flown into a windstorm
To be by your side, to embrace your face
but you had other plans
I would have carried both of us no matter how far
but you had other plans
I knew the one you loved and shared time with her
And as she left I knew that too. I just didn't know she loved you
and you loved her
and she left us on a summer day
I just didn't know she flew away
But I knew her when she was young
I cried for her and I cried for you.
I loved her and she broke my heart years ago
And now you have come to break it too
So many years ago she called me on the phone
To tell me she took my love
with laughter in the background
I felt myself floating
And you laugh at me too... and make sure I know you had other
plans
So now I belong to neither one of you
I ll burn sage to make the spirits leave
I don t care if you ever read this or know
How badly you broke my heart in every way
Walk the streets. Eat all the hearts
Just stay away from mine beloved
 I cried for you and died for you beloved
You don t need my fragile heart
Go find stronger people to laugh at and torment
I cried for you beloved
I cried for
you

Burn it down

There is no glory in my eyes
No answer for the days of wonder
I burned all my memories and
Burned all my feelings
You are gone
You are ashes
you are foam upon the ocean
You are glass on the floor after I dropped a glass with shards that
cut my feet
You aren't anything I want to hold on to
So go. There's no glory in goodbye
There is me and a match that I'm taking to your memory
I'm burning you down every time I think of you
I am burning you down. I can't take the thought of you
You are dust that floats upon the wind
You are the mist in the air
But you will bother me anymore
You have a crowd. I am not participating in a harem of lost souls
So off shall you go, to anywhere you want
Eat all the hearts but you will not have mine
It looks like I am there but I have left
Ghoul

Eat all the hearts, but I will take my little heart back

Nandeb hnaki bel frachat

It's not that unbelievable
But maybe it is
We weave our spells and tell our lies
And some never recover from the damage we do
So
Nandeb hnaki bel frachat
the ocean is deep
And I will not fish for you
I merely watch the havoc you wreak
Nandeb hnaki bel frachat
Nandeb hnaki bel frachat
The lives you destroy and the hearts you break
Laying scattered as you hunt your prey

Nandeb hnaki bel frachat

Ghost

with your haunted eyes and your sad stories
you re a mirage
Me, spinning all around, burning for you love made me a ghost

I am ghost
with arms all around me and you arent there
I am a ghost, with the pictures of you in my heart and in my mind
I am a ghost
I am a ghost of your eyes
I am a a ghost of your smile
I am ghost of everything you are

And now I am standing here
Wishing I could disappear
You kissed my scars
You told me they were ok
Then you turned around and left me crying
I am a ghost soaring above myself
I dare not call you I dare not speak your name
I dont want to hear your name
I am a ghost near the water.
I am a ghost when lovers kiss
I am a ghost in the doorway on the bed
I am the ghost that lay under you as you held my face
I am the ghost you left at the street

I am the ghost you dont know anymore

Antaya timbre fi

She told me that you hurt her
I did not say I knew you too
You lied to her and made her believe
That you would be there for her forever
She told me you took things from her
And told her lies when you knew all along you would never
marry her
Her innocence... you took it
You told her lies
I never told her I knew you too
You are a stamp beloved
Antaya timbre fi

Every girl knows you
I guess you thought you would wreck hearts and it would go
unpunished forever
But the chickens have come home to roost
All the lies are floating to the top of the ocean beloved

Antaya timbre fi

Burned you down

I lit a match to you and I
I burned us down at quarter to three
First I took a match to every conversation
Then I lit on fire the first place I kissed you
Then I burned down your voice, your face and your smile
I burned you down and then threw the ashes into water
Then I took your pictures, removed them from my mind and
buried you
I burned you down beloved
I learned to hate you like you deserve

I burned you all the way down
I did not need a voodoo doll to kill my love for you
I simply watched how awful you are as a person
Yes dear you are awful. Beyond redemption
So now as you feel your arms ache and your face get hot
That s the fire I threw you into as you angered me
Lie there and turn to dust , you despicable person
All that love became rage when you walked the streets and
looked for sweet hearts to destroy
So now you have voodoo and the rage of a thousand years of
memories and symbols etched
upon cairns

I lit a fire beneath you and curse the ground you walk on wicked
man
Until you stop your wicked ways
You will burn all the way to the ground because I deemed it so
In generational curse I call our grandparents to stop you
I call our blood lines to curse you
As I burn you all the way down

You feel the coldness of the earth around your shoulders?

That's my pagan curse for you. That's the call of the druids to
repel evil

You feel the sun beat too hot?
That's the time I left your photo on the driveway for the sun to
fade it
You never made me angry till I realized that you were on a path
to break people like you felt broken
So now my beloved you will burn.
You will burn and you will drown each day you wake up
Until you change your evil ways
You will burn and ache and feel tired without resting
You will suffer without ever understanding why
You met a bigger witch than you are a wizard or a druid

I will burn you all the way down

Zrigh elvadhnakh I know your secrets

But I will never tell
I know everything
But I will keep it safe with me
Ill never hurt or cause you harm
but
Zrigh elvadhnakh
yes beloved
Zrigh elvadhnakh
They are safe with me izem
Always safe with me
beloved

Zrigh elvadhnakh

Chemaa

You are the candle
And you dance across the walls as a shadow
and then the shadows grow
you are the candle
and hot as you burn.. you will one day cool
and I will hold my hands in front of my face in grief
when your love ends

when the night turns into dawn

You are the candle
whisper your smoke into the evening mist
as I open the window
and jasmine fills the room

You are the candle
And I disappear in your glow
as you break me

Dharbouh bel lahtab

like he never cared at all
dharbouh bel lahtab
He saw my tears and let them flow
and hit me with lumber until I fell into a deep sleep
He never loved me beloved and it was all a lie
We never loved at all
Then he became a phantom
I was left to drown in an ocean of his memories

dharbouh bel lahtab
I cried a thousand tears that no one could see
And because he lied to me, I could not see that it was futile
All I was was a joke and a game
And in the end he became a ghost and left me to drown alone
Far from shore
Never caring if I sunk
dharbouh bel lahtab

the last one to know beloved
I was the last one to know

You are a ghoul but not my ghoul

Darling beloved
You are a ghoul but not mine to fear
I can't bear the sight of you
But I am not afraid of you
I am not afraid of being close to you, monster
You just tore my heart in two
You just broke every part of me
It's our connection to the past
It's how much you loved her and how much you both hurt me
You are a ghoul but not my ghoul
You remain a ghost I cannot bear to see
My eyes fill with tears at the mention of your name
So be the ghost you need to be
Walk any street and look at everyone you want
I feel no fear from you
I know everything already and I just have never cared
I have seen bigger ghouls than you
I love you so
Just be that ghoul that you know how to be
And leave me in peace
I am already haunted on every level
All you do is add to my nightmares

www.ingramcontent.com/pod-product-compliance
Lightning Source LLC
Chambersburg PA
CBHW051846040426
42447CB00006B/716